BRITISH RAILWAYS

PAST and PRESENT

No 32

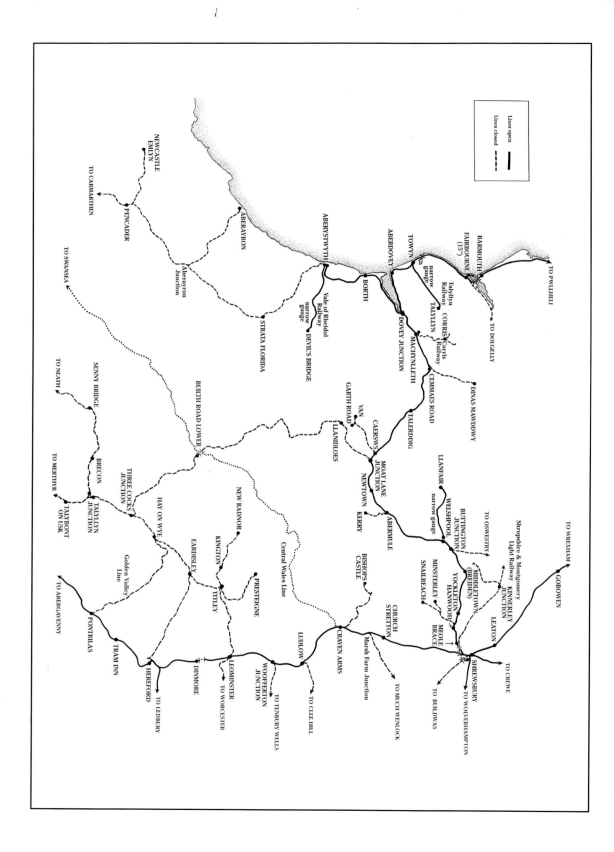

BRITISH RAILWAYS

PAST and PRESENT

No 32

Mid Wales and The Marches

Roger Siviter ARPS

Past and Present

Past & Present Publishing Ltd

First published in 1998
Reprinted 1999
Reprinted 2003

British Library Cataloguing in Publication Data

A catalogue record for this book is available from the British Library.

ISBN 1 85895 137 2

Past & Present Publishing Ltd
The Trundle
Ringstead Road
Great Addington
Kettering
Northants
NN14 4BW

Tel/Fax: 01536 330588
email: sales@nostalgiacollection.com
Website: www.nostalgiacollection.com

Maps drawn by Christina Siviter

Printed and bound in Great Britain

ACKNOWLEDGEMENTS

In compiling this book I have been helped by many people, and would like to thank the following: the staff at Past & Present Publishing Ltd; Lens of Sutton; my wife Christina; Michael Mensing; Hugh Ballantyne; all the photographers accredited herein; all the railwaymen who make it possible; and finally all the many people who kindly allowed me access to their land in order to obtain those sometimes elusive 'present' pictures.

BIBLIOGRAPHY

Britain's Light Railways *by Martin Smith (Ian Allan)*
Forgotten Railways: Volume 11, Severn Valley and Welsh Borders *by Rex Christiansen (David Charles)*
A Regional History of the Railways of Great Britain: Volume 11, North and Mid Wales *by Peter E. Baughan (David & Charles)*
Volume 13, Thames and Severn *by Rex Christiansen (David & Charles)*

Branch Line Byways: Volume 1, The West Midlands *by G. F. Bannister (Atlantic Transport Publishers)*
The Welsh Marches *by Roger Siviter (Baton Transport)*

The Railway Magazine
Railway World
Trains Illustrated

CONTENTS

TALERDDIG BANK: High summer on the Cambrian main line, and BR Standard Class '4MT' 4-6-0 No 75002 has steam to spare as it approaches the summit of Talerddig bank with a lightweight Machynlleth to Shrewsbury local train on the afternoon of 20 August 1966. The ex-GWR 'Manor' Class 4-6-0s had finished work at the end of 1965, but the Standard '4MT' 4-6-0s and 2-6-0s were to carry on working on the Cambrian lines until 4 March 1967, when the through workings from Paddington to Shrewsbury came to an end. *RS*

INTRODUCTION

The old GWR route from Gobowen to Shrewsbury (part of the line from Paddington to Chester) is the starting point for our journey. The Cambrian routes from Oswestry to Buttington Junction and their branches will be covered in the 'Past and Present' volume on North Wales, as will the lines north of Barmouth and east to Bala Junction and Ruabon, etc.

From Shrewsbury (after looking at the Shropshire & Montgomeryshire Light Railway) we take the former Great Western Railway/London & North Western Railway (GWR&LNWR) Joint line south to Hereford and Pontrilas, then take in some of the branch lines on the western side of the route, including the GWR Kington branch, the Midland branch to Three Cocks Junction, and on to Talyllyn Junction, Brecon and Talybont-on-Usk on the Brecon & Merthyr Railway.

After a short interlude showing some of the fine preserved locomotives that have worked in the area – Hereford saw the start of the return of main-line steam in October 1971, mainly thanks to the efforts of Bulmers – we return to Shrewsbury and travel this time to Welshpool, Dovey Junction and Barmouth to the north, then to Aberystwyth in the south, taking in the cross-country route from Moat Lane Junction via Llanidloes to Three Cocks Junction. Also covered are some of the narrow-gauge lines of the area and the 15-inch-gauge Fairbourne Railway. From Aberystwyth we travel south towards Carmarthen, calling at Aberayron, and our journey ends at Pencader, the junction for Newcastle Emlyn.

I have many fond memories of the lovely areas covered by this book, starting with a wartime holiday in 1943 at Clun. This journey started at Birmingham Snow Hill station, and I well remember our train to Shrewsbury appearing from Snow Hill Tunnel as if out of nowhere and scaring me to death with its sheer sound and size (I was only six at the time). I have no idea what locomotive was on the train, but it could have been a 'King' or 'Castle', or even a 'Star' or 'Saint' Class 4-6-0. From Shrewsbury we travelled down the Joint route to Craven Arms, then by bus to Clun – and, yes, we did remember our ration books!

On to August 1951 and, after a week's holiday at Tenby, I persuaded my father to return to the Birmingham area via Aberystwyth, where we called in at the station for me to take a few numbers and make a short trip. Reproduced here is the ticket I bought at the station for a return journey to Borth; it looks as if I was able to persuade the guard not to clip it. Note that they were still issuing GWR tickets even in 1951. Also reproduced here is a page from my Ian Allan locospotter's book, showing that I saw four 'Dukedog' '9000' Class 4-4-0s

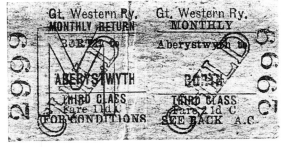

4-4-0   9000 Class

Introduced 1936.
Weights : Loco.   49 tons 0 cwt.
           Tender 40 tons 0 cwt.
Pressure :   180 lb.   Cyls.: 18″ × 26″
Driving Wheels: 5′ 8″   T.E.: 18,955 lb.

9000	9009	9016	9024
9001	9010	9017	9025
9002	9011	9018	9026
9003	9012	9020	9027
9004	9013	9021	9028
9005	9014	9022	
9008	9015	9023	

Total 26

that day, a Class that I had never seen before or since. According to the Ian Allan *Locoshed Book* of the period, Nos 9001 and 9016 were from Oswestry shed (89A), 9009 and 9025 being from 89C Machynlleth, of which Aberystwyth was a sub-shed. Also interesting to note is that at the time, of the 26 locomotives, only Nos 9008, 9010, 9011, 9015, 9018 and 9023 were shedded outside the Cambrian area.

In March 1955, during my Army service with the Band of the Worcestershire Regiment, we spent a fortnight with the TA regiment at Sennybridge camp near Brecon, which meant an interesting trip by special troop train from Worcester Shrub Hill to Hereford, then via the Midland route from Hereford to Three Cocks Junction, and via Talyllyn Junction and Brecon (on the Brecon & Merthyr Railway) to Devynock & Sennybridge station, this last section being on the Neath & Brecon Railway – quite a journey! Incidentally, the camp (unlike some) was very near the station, which meant only a short march – thank goodness!

In 1966, when I had started photographing the end of BR steam, I spent many happy hours at Shrewsbury and on the Cambrian route (see *Classic Steam: 1966* published by Silver Link Publishing Ltd). Especially memorable was a visit to Talerddig bank on Saturday 20 August, when the sun shone all day and on the radio was the commentary on an exciting test match between England and the West Indies. Happy memories!

Also memorable was the sound of English Electric Class 37s roaring up the 1 in 52 of Talerddig bank. Alas, this is very rare nowadays, 'Sprinter' units having replaced them.

Finally, in latter years, thanks to the efforts of many enthusiasts and the Friends of the Main Line Steam Operators, there have been steam trips over the Marches and Cambrian routes, thus keeping alive the spirit of steam in what for me must surely be one of the most beautiful parts of the British Isles.

Roger Siviter
Bromsgrove

Gobowen and Shrewsbury

GOBOWEN 1: Our journey begins at Gobowen, some 17 miles north-west of Shrewsbury on the Paddington to Chester main line. Gobowen was the junction for the line to Oswestry and Buttington Junction where it joined the line from Shrewsbury to the Cambrian Coast via Machynlleth. Although these lines closed in the 1960s, a section of the line from Gobowen to Blodwell Junction was kept open to obtain ballast for rail use. Blodwell is situated some 5 miles south of Oswestry on a loop off the line to Buttington, and was the junction station for Llangynog, some 10 miles to the west.

The 'past' scene, taken from the north-west around the turn of the century, shows the fine station buildings and presumably all the staff at the time. On the right-hand side can be seen the bay platform for the Oswestry line.

The scene at Gobowen on 25 February 1998 shows that the station building (now listed) survives, although today it is used for office accommodation. The old-fashioned lamps make an elegant addition. *Lens of Sutton/RS*

GOBOWEN (2): On 3 January 1985 diesel multiple unit (DMU) No 53312 enters the station with the 1040 Shrewsbury to Chester train. Although this picture was taken only 13 years ago, most of the infrastructure is the same as in the 1950s and '60s, with the GWR footbridge, station canopies and GWR bench on the left-hand side being particularly notable. The extensive sidings on the left were for use by quarry trains.

The two 'present' photographs, taken on 25 February 1998, show that much has changed since 1985. The first shows a typical freight working of the area, Class 56 No 56087 heading north with the 0605 Margam to Dee Marsh loaded steel coil train. The second picture shows two-car DMU set No 150121 forming the 1117 Birmingham New Street to Chester service. These trains run on a two-hour basis (each way) and it is hoped in the future to make this an hourly service.

Comparisons with the earlier picture show that the footbridge has now gone (although it is planned to reinstate it), as have the sidings and signal box on the left-hand side; note, however, the original nameboard, the booking office, which is now run by Moreton Hall Travel, and the neat fencing. The 150th anniversary of the line to Oswestry and Welshpool fell in 1998, and it was hoped to commemorate this with a suitable event. *All RS*

GOBOWEN (3): Also photographed on 3 January 1985 was Class 25 No 25300 as it approached the station from the south with empty stone wagons for Blodwell quarry. Sister locomotive No 25303 can just be seen to the left of the impressive GWR signal box, waiting to head south with a full ballast train. On the right-hand side is the junction to Blodwell quarry. Note the mixture of upper and lower quadrant signals.

At the same spot on 25 February 1998 we see the rear of the 1128 Chester to Birmingham New Street service ('Sprinter' unit No 156422) heading for Shrewsbury. Although the quarry traffic has now ceased, the junction for the line can be seen just beyond the coal wagon, which is on a siding leading to the small coal depot. As stated earlier, the signal box, semaphore signals and sidings have now gone, together with the Class 25 locomotives. *Both RS*

13

NEAR HAUGHTON: In the mid-1960s the trains between Shrewsbury and Chester were still steam-hauled, and on 2 August 1966 Class '5' 4-6-0 No 45231 runs through pleasant rural surroundings near Haughton, 12 miles north of Shrewsbury, with a midday Chester to Shrewsbury train.

Apart from the traction, very little appears to have changed by 25 February 1998. The train is the 1328 Chester to Birmingham New Street service, formed of unit No 150121. The background to the location is a former wartime airfield, which reverted to farming after the war. *Both RS*

LEATON: On 23 April 1966 Class '5' 4-6-0 No 44856 approaches Leaton, some 4 miles north of Shrewsbury, with a heavy midday southbound freight. The locomotive has a Nuneaton (2B) shed code, so the train could be heading for that area. *RS*

Opposite page The first view of Leaton signal box, crossing and (closed) station was taken on 5 August 1978, looking towards Chester. Almost two decades later, on 25 February 1998, the station building and crossing house are still there, but the signal box has gone and a modern barrier crossing has replaced the old gates. *Michael Mensing/RS*

COTON HILL: Our next location is on the outskirts of Shrewsbury at Coton Hill, and the photograph shows the very busy-looking Greenfields goods depot. The date is 25 October 1966 and the approaching train is the 3.30pm from Shrewsbury to Birkenhead, hauled by Class '5' 4-6-0 No 45132. In the background can be seen the line from Shrewsbury to Crewe, this area being known as Crewe Bank; also dominating the background is Shrewsbury prison.

Greenfields goods depot has now disappeared and part of it is used as a car park. By 25 February 1998 one of the tracks on the Chester line has been taken up, but some semaphore signals still remain in use, and there is a signal box at the north end of Shrewsbury station, out of sight behind the bushes on the right-hand side. Many buildings still remain, including the prison and the imposing clock tower. On the line to Crewe can be seen a single-car DMU forming the 1550 Shrewsbury to Chester service. *Both RS*

SHREWSBURY (1): Standard Class '4MT' No 75029 has just brought the up 'Cambrian Coast Express' into platform 4 at Shrewsbury station on 29 October 1966. Within a few minutes a Brush Class 47 diesel locomotive will couple on to the other end of the train and head south for Wolverhampton Low Level, Birmingham Snow Hill and London Paddington. No 75029 will then go down to Shrewsbury shed (south of the station on the line to Hereford) for servicing before its next turn of duty.

No 75029 is now preserved by the artist David Shepherd on the East Somerset Railway at Cranmore and is named *The Green Knight*. The modern locomotive, seen on 6 August 1994 a few yards back from the previous view, is Class 47 No 47745 with a special Pullman train heading for Crewe. The station still retains its platform canopies and buildings and also its very fine-looking chimneys. The water column has gone but the pedestrian bridge that spans the whole of the station is still there. At one time the station boasted an overall roof, but this was removed in 1963. *Both RS*

SHREWSBURY (2): Looking north out of the station we can see the signal gantry and overhead trolley bridge with its lift tower. The Chester line is straight ahead, while the Crewe route swings away to the right. The roof of the goods office for Greenfield depot can just be seen to the right of the locomotive, ex-LMS Class '8F' 2-8-0 No 48738, which is heading north in the Crewe direction with a mixed freight on 25 October 1966.

In the second view, some 19 years later on 24 May 1985, a Class 08 diesel shunter is approaching the station from the Chester line with the empty stock of a southbound steam special to be hauled by 'Castle' Class 4-6-0 No 7029 *Clun Castle*. The goods office is still there, as are most of the semaphore signals. The lines from Crewe can be seen clearly, coming in from the right of the picture. There is also some change in the trackwork.

Much remains the same today. On 25 February 1998 the train is the rear of the 1517 Birmingham New Street to Chester service, formed by 'Sprinter' unit No 156404. Colour light signals have replaced all but one of the semaphores on the gantry and, compared to the 1966 view, some of the pointwork has disappeared. The gantry on the Crewe line has been replaced by a bracket signal, and the goods office has gone, replaced by a new warehouse-type building. On the extreme left-hand side can be seen the edge of the signal box that controls this area. *All RS*

SHREWSBURY (3): As stated before, Shrewsbury's overall roof was removed in 1963, but this picture of ex-GWR 'Manor' Class 4-6-0 No 7818 *Granville Manor* waiting to leave with the 3.50pm to Aberystwyth on 5 August 1961 shows the station as it was before the removal of the roof.

On 25 February 1998, DMU No 150121 has just arrived at platform 5 with the 1537 from Birmingham New Street. The overall roof has been replaced by canopies, but the station buildings are still there. *Michael Mensing/RS*

SHREWSBURY (4): On 7 May 1966 Class '5MT' No 44775 waits while the vans are filled with parcels at platform 3. Note the advertisement for that year's football World Cup. The scene gives a good view of the station architecture of this former joint GWR/LMS station.

Today platform 3 is rarely used for passenger trains, but this view, taken on 25 February 1998, shows that much of the fine station architecture remains. *Both RS*

SHREWSBURY (5): There is not a 'Visivest' to be seen as BR Standard 4-6-0 No 75016 departs from Shrewsbury's platform 4 at 2.15pm with the down 'Cambrian Coast Express'. At Dovey Junction, west of Machynlleth, the train will split, one portion going to Aberystwyth and the other to Barmouth and Pwllheli.

The present view shows the 1325 service to Aberystwyth (1217 from Birmingham New Street) leaving platform 4 on 6 August 1994; the 'Sprinter' unit is No 156419. Some of platform 3 and the relevant trackwork, as well as the station nameboard, have disappeared, but the bracket signal (now upper-quadrant) is still there, and so is Shrewsbury prison! Bay platform 2, which shared platform 3 at this point, has gone, and bay platform 1 is now closed, the trackwork for both having been taken up. *Both RS*

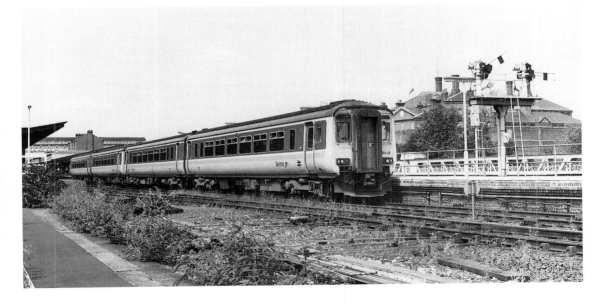

SHREWSBURY (6): The first view is a three-quarter rear shot of No 75016 leaving the station with the down 'Cambrian Coast Express' on 25 October 1966 (see the picture on the previous page).

On 23 April 1966, the date of the second view, 4-6-0 No 75012 reverses into platform 4 in order to take out the down 'Cambrian'. This is a similar angle to the previous picture but shows more clearly the famous London & North Western Railway (LNWR) signal box (which is now a listed building), Shrewsbury Abbey, and the junction of the Wolverhampton lines (to the left of the signal box) with the Hereford and Cambrian lines, and also the Severn Valley line. Also seen is the water tower situated at the end of platform 4.

Today's scene shows the same location with 'Sprinter' No 158816 departing with the 1333 Manchester Piccadilly to Cardiff service on 6 August 1994. The water tower has now gone, as have the lines that led to platform 3, this platform having been shortened. The junction line to Wolverhampton can be seen under the coaches. *All RS*

SHREWSBURY MPD: To the south of Shrewsbury station and situated to the east of the Hereford and Cambrian lines was Shrewsbury locomotive shed. There were originally two sheds on this site, GWR and LMS (Shrewsbury being a joint station), but both sheds later came under Western Region control, with shed code 84G (then 89A). With boundary changes in 1963, the shed moved to London Midland Region control, and the code became 6D. Pictured in the yard on 23 April 1966 are ex-GWR 'Manor' Class 4-6-0s Nos 7812 *Erlestoke Manor* and 7820 *Dinmore Manor*, both now preserved. Behind the 'Manors' are BR Standard Class '5MT' 4-6-0 No 73125 (fitted with Caprotti valve gear) and an unidentified 'Black Five' 4-6-0. I was unable to get the Peugeot car moved, but arguably it provides a contrast with the locomotives and an interesting period piece to modern eyes. The shed closed in 1967, and the second view shows the site of the yard on 17 February 1998. *Both RS*

Sutton Bridge Junction

SUTTON BRIDGE JUNCTION (1): This photograph of the down 'Cambrian Coast Express' approaching Sutton Bridge Junction signal box on 28 May 1966, with 4-6-0 No 75006 in charge, gives a good view of Shrewsbury shed and yard. The shed turntable is on the right-hand side of the picture, out of sight behind the signal box. The Severn Valley line can be seen swinging away behind the signal box.

Nowadays, to copy the previous picture you have to include the new footbridge that spans the line immediately north of the signal box. This was the scene on 6 August 1994 as 'Sprinter' unit No 158786 takes the Cambrian line with the 1617 Birmingham New Street to Aberystwyth service. Note that the junction is now adjacent to the signal box, whereas in the previous picture it was situated some yards south of the road bridge on which I was standing. *Both RS*

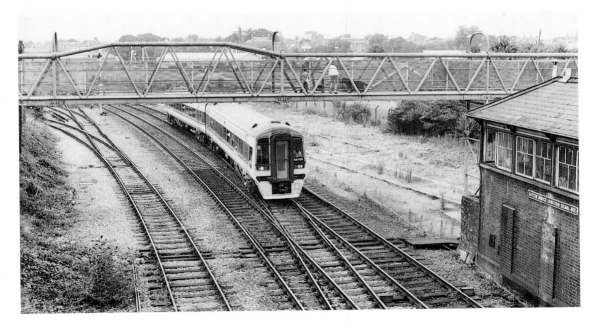

SUTTON BRIDGE JUNCTION (2): These four views were taken from the footbridge seen in the last picture – views not possible in earlier days. The first, dated 28 January 1984, shows Class 33 No 33039 with the 1003 Crewe to Cardiff train. On the left, by the single line tablet-catching equipment, is Class 08 shunter No 08686. Note also the former shed area in the background.

By the mid-1980s the 'Crompton' Class 33s had been superseded on the Crewe-Cardiff service by the Class 37s, and on the evening of 15 July 1989 No 37408 is seen approaching Sutton Bridge Junction with the 1838 Shrewsbury to Cardiff train (1715 from Liverpool Lime Street).

The third photograph shows a re-enactment of BR steam days as, on a very wet 29 September 1991, BR Standard Class '4MT' 4-6-0 No 75069 heads west for Aberystwyth with the 'Cambrian Limited'.

Nearly all Hereford ('North & West') line and Cambrian line trains are now operated by 'Sprinter' units. The 'present' picture at Sutton Bridge was taken on 17 February 1998 and shows the 1459 Manchester Piccadilly to Cardiff service formed by unit No 158842. A comparison with the previous three pictures shows changes to the trackwork and semaphore signals, as well as many changes to the background where the locomotive shed and yard were. *All RS*

SUTTON BRIDGE JUNCTION (3): The down 'Cambrian' once again, on 28 May 1966 (the old Whit Saturday), as No 75006 takes the Cambrian line to Welshpool and beyond. The North & West line to Hereford stretches out straight ahead, and the bridge in the distance carried the Shropshire & Montgomeryshire Light Railway (S&M), which ran westwards to Llanymynech, where it connected with the Cambrian line from Whitchurch and Oswestry to Buttington Junction, thence to Welshpool and the Cambrian Coast. Although for the sake of simplification I use the term 'Cambrian line' from Shrewsbury, it was as far as Buttington Junction a GWR/LNWR Joint line. The Shrewsbury terminus of the S&M was the Abbey station, adjacent to that historic building, and the line ran to the east of the locomotive depot before swinging westwards over the bridge seen here.

On 17 February 1998 Class 60 No 60088 passes Sutton Bridge Junction with the 1110 Margam-Dee Marsh steel coil train. The sidings on the left have gone and the Cambrian line on the right singled, but the semaphore signals still remain. *Both RS*

33

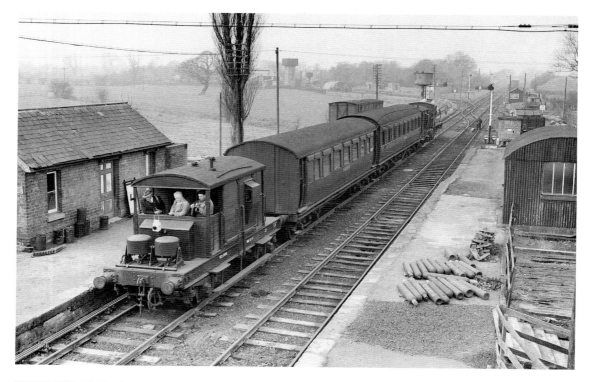

KINNERLEY (S&M): On 20 March 1960 the Stephenson Locomotive Society (SLS) ran a last-day special on the Shropshire & Montgomeryshire Light Railway, which is seen at Kinnerley (the main point on the railway) with Austerity 0-6-0 tank locomotive No 193, built by Hunslet in 1953, in charge. Kinnerley was the junction for the only branch on the line, to Criggion. The train is facing towards Llanymynech, and the Criggion branch can be seen swinging away to the left past the locomotive shed, just visible in the top centre of the picture.

The line was opened in 1866 and had a chequered career, closing in 1880 and opening again in 1909. Probably its most famous period was in the 1920s, when it was run by Colonel Stephens (of Kent & East Sussex renown). It was taken over by the War Department in 1941 and finally closed on 29 February 1960.

The same view on 31 March 1998 is somewhat obscured, but I can confirm that, out of sight behind the foliage, the water tower seen in the top centre of the past picture is still there, and some of the WD buildings and half of the wall of the station building on the left-hand side survive. *Hugh Ballantyne/RS*

SUTTON BRIDGE JUNCTION: Returning to the Hereford line at Sutton Bridge, we see preserved ex-LNWR Webb Class '2F' 0-6-2 'Coal Tank' No 1054 and support coach heading for Shrewsbury on 18 October 1986 to take out a special train to Chester and beyond in celebration of the 80th birthday of the famous railway and tramways historian and photographer W. A. Camwell, or 'Cam' as he was affectionately known. By this time the Cambrian line had been singled, but the sidings on the left were still in use.

The second photograph of the same location gives a clearer view of the junction as Class 37 No 37719 (deputising for 'Castle' Class 4-6-0 No 5080 *Defiant*) heads for Shrewsbury with a special charter train from Hereford on 15 April 1989. *Both RS*

North & West route: Shrewsbury to Hereford

BAYSTON HILL, SHREWSBURY: On leaving the medieval town of Shrewsbury, Hereford-bound trains are faced with an almost continuous climb to Church Stretton, some 13 miles to the south. On 10 June 1989 ex-GWR 'Modified Hall' Class 4-6-0 No 6998 *Burton Agnes Hall* is seen climbing the 1 in 127 up Bayston Hill, just 2 miles south of Shrewsbury. The train is a return special from Shrewsbury to Newport.

In less than 10 years a radical change has occurred. A new bypass (the A5 trunk route to North Wales) has been built to relieve the heavy congestion on the old bypass, which was carried by the road bridge seen clearly in the 'past' picture and just visible under the new bypass bridge in the 'present' one, taken on 17 February 1998. The train in today's scene is the 1433 Manchester Piccadilly to Cardiff service, which takes 3 hours 12 minutes for the 169.75-mile journey. *Both RS*

DORRINGTON: On 20 May 1978 ex-LMS 'Pacific' No 6201 *Princess Elizabeth* approaches the remains of Dorrington station (6 miles south of Shrewsbury) with a southbound special from Chester. Although the station closed in the 1950s, much of it remains intact, including the fine-looking station house. Note also the staggered platforms, and the loop and siding running in front of the signal box.

By 17 February 1998 all the station buildings have gone and only a bit of the old platform remains to serve as a reminder that there was once a station at this location, although the signal box, some semaphore signals and a siding survive from the past days. A new factory complex has appeared on the right-hand side. *Both RS*

ALL STRETTON HALT: At one time the Church Stretton area could boast three stations. As well as the main one at Church Stretton itself, just to the north was All Stretton Halt, while just south of the main station was Little Stretton Halt. On 10 June 1957, Whit Monday, ex-LMS 'Jubilee' Class 4-6-0 No 45689 *Ajax* passes the northbound platform of All Stretton Halt with the all-stations 3.55pm Shrewsbury to Hereford train. At this point there is a road bridge giving access to the halt, on the other side of which is the southbound platform.

Just over 40 years later, on 17 February 1998, 'Sprinter' No 158838 passes the site of the Halt with the 1333 Manchester Piccadilly to Cardiff service. *Michael Mensing/RS*

CHURCH STRETTON: On the evening of 10 June 1957 Standard Class '5' 4-6-0 No 73134 pulls through Church Stretton station with an afternoon extra train from Liverpool to Cardiff.

Today's view, taken on 17 February 1998, shows another train from Liverpool, this time the 1300 Liverpool-Bristol service, comprising 'Sprinter' unit No 158824 – a far cry from the 14 coaches in the previous picture! The old station buildings have given way to a modern 'bus shelter', but the footbridge remains, albeit with the roof removed. Note also the signal box beyond the bridge and the semaphore signals; these are still a feature of the North & West route. *Michael Mensing/RS*

MARSHBROOK: Some 3 miles south of Church Stretton was the station of Marshbrook, situated on the southern tip of the Long Mynd that stretches just to the north and west of Church Stretton. With the Long Mynd as a backdrop, ex-LMS Fowler Class '4' 2-6-4 tank No 42305 passes through Marshbrook station on 10 June 1957 with the 2.45pm Shrewsbury to Swansea Victoria train (via the Central Wales line).

The 'present' view shows 'Sprinter' unit No 158828 passing the site of Marshbrook station on 17 February 1998 with the 1233 Manchester Piccadilly to Swansea via Newport service. The station has long since gone but the station house is still there, together with the signal box and semaphore signals, although the signal dominating the scene is a comparatively new addition. *Michael Mensing/RS*

CRAVEN ARMS: South of Marshbrook and just over 3 miles north of Craven Arms was Marsh Farm Junction, where the line to Much Wenlock, Buildwas Junction and Wellington joined the North & West route (this line is featured in the 'Past and Present Companion' on the Severn Valley Railway). Also nearby was the junction for the Bishop's Castle line, which ran north-westwards for 9.5 miles from Stretford Bridge Junction, about three-quarters of a mile north of Craven Arms & Stokesay station. This line opened in 1865 and closed in 1935.

On 6 October 1979 ex-GWR 'King' Class 4-6-0 No 6000 *King George V* approaches Craven Arms with a southbound special made up of the Didcot Railway Museum's GWR chocolate-and-cream coaching stock. This was one of the final runs with these GWR coaches before retirement a few months later. The GWR footbridge is still intact and there are still sidings and a goods shed. The small locomotive shed was to the south and west of the goods shed; a sub-shed of Shrewsbury, it closed in the mid-1960s.

The scene on 17 February 1998 shows Class 60 No 60019 approaching Craven Arms with the 0902 Dee Marsh-Margam empty steel train. The fine GWR footbridge has gone, replaced by a new bridge nearer the southern end of the platforms. The old goods shed, signal box and semaphore signals still remain, although most of the sidings are have been removed, as well as the buildings on the right-hand side where houses now stand.

Just south of Craven Arms station is the junction for the Central Wales line, also the subject of a 'Past & Present Companion'. *Both RS*

LUDLOW: Eight miles south of Craven Arms is the fine old medieval town of Ludlow, served by a station on the higher ground just west of the town centre. This view, looking north, was taken in the early 1960s, and shows the small goods yard and goods shed as well as the station buildings. Just to the north of Ludlow was the junction for the quarry line to Clee Hill to the east, and just above this junction were water troughs.

This view of Ludlow station on 22 February 1998 shows that the old station building has been replaced by a modern 'bus shelter'. The goods yard has long gone but the goods building survives, although now used for other purposes. *Lens of Sutton/RS*

WOOFFERTON JUNCTION: On 10 June 1957 ex-GWR '5700' Class 0-6-0 pannier tank No 4641 arrives at this splendidly named country junction station with the 6.25pm train from Kidderminster via Bewdley, Cleobury Mortimer and Tenbury Wells. What a delightful journey that must have been, even more so on what appears to have been a lovely summer's evening. The Tenbury line can be glimpsed swinging away eastwards in front of the signal box on the left-hand side of the picture. (For more pictures of this fascinating branch, and the whole of the Severn Valley line, see my 'Past & Present Companion' on the SVR.)

It was not possible to take the present picture from the same angle as the past. However, this view, taken on 2 September 1994, shows that although the station has now gone, the station house, goods shed and signal box are still there; however, the line to Tenbury and Bewdley closed completely in 1965. The train, 'Sprinter' unit No 158823, is the 1433 Manchester Piccadilly to Cardiff Central service. *Michael Mensing/RS*

LEOMINSTER is our next location on the North & West route. This view, looking south, was taken in the early 1960s and shows Leominster's famous elevated signal box.

Alas, in today's view, taken in the late afternoon of 22 February 1998, we see that the signal box has gone. Also, Leominster is now no longer the junction station for Worcester to the east and Kington branches to the west, these lines having disappeared with the Beeching closures in the mid-1960s. The station now serves just a through route, with two platforms instead of the four in the 'past' picture, although the northbound platform still retains the platform buildings and canopy. *Lens of Sutton/RS*

DINMORE TUNNEL is some 6 miles north of Hereford. Here at the southern end we see the 3.30pm Manchester to Plymouth and Paignton train hauled by ex-GWR 'Hall' Class 4-6-0 No 5998 *Trevor Hall*.

On 22 February 1998 'Sprinter' unit No 158303 is seen at the same location with the 1332 Crewe-Cardiff train. Apart from the disappearance of the platelayer's hut and the 'catch points' sign at the tunnel mouth, and concrete sleepers replacing the wooden ones, little appears to have changed. *Michael Mensing/RS*

HEREFORD (1): On 2 June 1979 ex-LMS Class '5' 4-6-0 pulls out of Hereford station with the first leg – Hereford to Shrewsbury – of the 'Midlander' rail tour, which later ran south to Hereford and Newport before returning to Hereford. At the time this locomotive was on loan to the Severn Valley Railway from the National Collection, and this was its first passenger run on BR since restoration.

At the same place on 22 February 1998 it can be seen that some sidings have gone, as well as the old goods shed on the left-hand side. The train is the 1305 Cardiff to Crewe and Liverpool/Manchester service with 'Sprinter' unit No 158835. On the through line in the station itself is Class 60 No 60083 at the head of the 1056 (Sundays) Margam-Dee Marsh steel coil train. *Both RS*

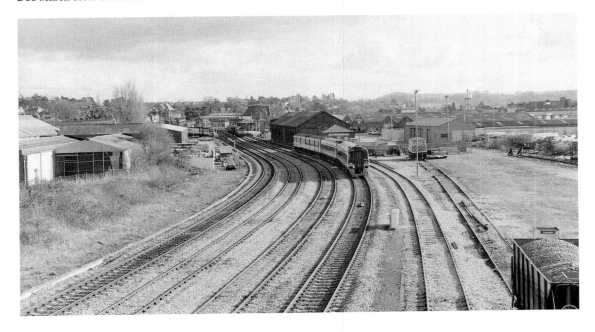

HEREFORD (2): Ex-GWR '2251' Class 0-6-0 No 2249 pulls out of Barrs Court station, Hereford, with the 4.30pm to Gloucester on 18 August 1962. The Hereford to Gloucester line closed in 1965 under the Beeching Plan, while the Hereford to Eardisley, Hay and Brecon line had closed completely by 1964.

Nineteen years later, on the evening of 2 October 1981, Class 33 No 33031 pulls out of Hereford with a Crewe-Cardiff train. These Type 3 diesels were introduced in 1960 and became known as 'Cromptons' simply because they were fitted with four Crompton-Parkinson 305hp axle-hung nose-suspended traction motors. They worked on the North & West route from the late 1970s until the mid-1980s. In the background, waiting to leave for Newport, is a very famous locomotive, ex-GWR 'King' Class 4-6-0 No 6000 *King George V*, hauling a steam special to commemorate the 10th anniversary of the return of steam to BR, a train that No 6000 had hauled from Hereford on 2 October 1971. The return had been brought about mainly by the efforts of Bulmers Ltd, and in particular Peter Prior.

To complete this trio of pictures we see ex-GWR 'King' Class No 6024 *King Edward I* pulling out of Hereford and heading for Newport to celebrate the 25th anniversary of the return of steam on 2 October 1996. Nowadays, steam specials are common on the main line, thanks in no small way to the above-mentioned, and also to the Steam Locomotive Operators Association (SLOA), which has carried on the good work now for approaching 30 years.

In all three pictures can be seen the signal box at the southern end of the station. In the first picture it is named Ayleston Hill, but now it is called just Hereford. Today the sidings have long gone and the semaphore signals have been replaced by colour lights. *Michael Mensing/RS (2)*

HEREFORD MPD (86C) was situated on the west side of the avoiding goods line by Barton goods yard. Because the North & West route was a former GWR/LMS Joint line, it was common to see locomotives of both companies on shed, as in this picture taken on 18 August 1962. Ex-LMS rebuilt 'Royal Scot' Class 4-6-0 No 46118 *Royal Welch Fusilier* stands alongside ex-GWR '2800' Class 2-8-0 No 3841, two very handsome locomotives indeed. Both also have Swindon influence; the '2800' was designed by Churchward and built at Swindon, while the 'Royal Scot', originally a Fowler LMS design, was redesigned and rebuilt by Stanier, who spent his early years at Swindon.

The shed is no longer with us, and the avoiding line is now a walkway. In its place is an office block and factory complex. *Michael Mensing/RS*

TRAM INN station was some 5 miles south of Hereford. On Easter Monday, 7 April 1958, Standard Class '4' 4-6-0 No 75021 hurries over the crossing with the 9.45am Birmingham Snow Hill to Cardiff train.

The station has now gone and in consequence it was not possible to take today's picture from the end of the platform; it was taken instead from the garden wall of the Tram Inn itself, by kind permission of Mrs M. Cochrane. The train is the 0916 Liverpool Lime Street to Cardiff service, formed of 'Sprinter' unit No 158834, and the date is 4 March 1998. The signal box and semaphore signal are still there, but new crossing barriers have replaced the old gates, and the goods shed on the left is now part of a garage complex. *Michael Mensing/RS*

PONTRILAS: The final picture in this section is a view of Pontrilas station, looking north, taken around the end of the last century. The 'Golden Valley' line to Hay-on-Wye can be seen swinging away westwards just above the signal box in the centre of the picture. There is much to enjoy in this picture, including a donkey cart, a steam traction engine, people in period dress, a steam crane, a variety of goods wagons, and the Victorian railway infrastructure; note also the 'Golden Valley' branch train in the bay platform, and the wood yard on the left.

Today's scene, photographed on 4 March 1998, still shows many similarities with its Victorian predecessor. The station building is still there, although now in use as a private residence, and the houses on the left of the picture also survive. The 'Golden Valley' route has long been closed, but there is still a signal box and semaphore signals in the same positions. Passenger services were withdrawn from Pontrilas in 1958 with the Western Region's withdrawal of local passenger services between Shrewsbury, Hereford and Newport. *Lens of Sutton/RS*

Branches from Leominster to Brecon

KINGTON: Our first destination is on what was known as the ex-GWR Kington branches, which stretched as far as New Radnor, 19 miles to the west of Leominster. Just before Kington itself there was a 7-mile branch heading north from Titley Junction to Presteigne. Also at Titley Junction there was a line to the south to Eardisley on the Midland Railway route from Hereford to Hay-on-Wye, but this connection was closed in 1940.

On 27 July 1957 a special train, organised by the SLS, was run to celebrate the Leominster-Kington centenary. It comprised ex-GWR '1400' Class 0-4-2 tank No 1455 and auto-trailers Nos W243W and W242W, and is seen taking water at Kington station after arriving from Leominster. The Kington branches were all closed by 1964.

The view today, photographed on 7 March 1998, shows the site of the station, which is now a factory estate. However, the goods shed, the edge of which can be seen on the right-hand side of the 'present' picture, is now in use as a garage. *Hugh Ballantyne/RS*

EARDISLEY, on the Hereford to Hay line, is our next location. This line opened in 1864 and was known as the Hereford, Hay & Brecon Railway (HH&B). It was taken over by the Midland Railway in 1874 and subsequently by the LMS, finally closing in 1964. The line from Titley Junction on the Kington branch joined this line just to the east of Eardisley. On 6 June 1960 Class '2MT' 2-6-0 No 46506 pauses at the station with the 10.25am from Brecon to Hereford. This picture is a splendid reminder of the country branch line scene in steam days, sadly now gone.

A look at today's picture, taken on 4 March 1998, shows that the goods shed and office are still there and in commercial use, and that a modern bungalow occupies almost the identical location of the old wooden station building, which, long after closure, was dismantled and is now the station building at Raven Square, Welshpool, on the Welshpool & Llanfair Light Railway. *Hugh Ballantyne/RS*

HAY-ON-WYE was where the Midland line from Hereford met the GWR 'Golden Valley' line from Pontrilas, which opened in 1889, closed to passengers in 1941 and finally closed in the 1960s. We see a busy scene at the station on 10 June 1960; on the right is the 4.05pm from Hereford to Brecon, hauled again by 2-6-0 No 46506, and on the left is the rear of the 4.10pm Brecon to Hereford train, hauled by ex-GWR '5700' Class 0-6-0 pannier tank No 3662.

The whole of the site of Hay-on-Wye station is now a country superstore, the rear of which can be seen in the 'present' picture, taken on 4 March 1998. On the extreme left of the picture can be glimpsed the River Wye, the only identifying feature shared with the 'past' picture. *Hugh Ballantyne/RS*

THREE COCKS JUNCTION: Heading south-west from Hay we come to this quaintly named station, where the Cambrian line from Moat Lane Junction, Llanidloes and Builth Wells (featured later in this book) met the Hereford to Brecon line, then ran to Talyllyn Junction. On a very cold 29 December 1962 (the start of the 'big freeze') Class '2MT' 2-6-0s Nos 46518 and 46505 are coupled tender-to-tender to haul the very last 11.15am train to Builth Road Lower. On the right, out of sight, were the platforms for the Hereford to Brecon line.

The site of Three Cocks Junction is now part of an industrial estate, as this picture, taken on 4 March 1998, clearly shows. On the right-hand side can be seen the foundations of the station buildings featured in the 'past' picture, which, according to a reliable local source, had been demolished only in the last few years. *Hugh Ballantyne/RS*

TALYLLYN JUNCTION, some 8 miles south of Three Cocks, was where the Brecon line swung away to the west, and the line to Merthyr and Newport continued to the south. On 28 December 1962 ex-GWR 0-6-0 pannier tank No 9616 leaves the Newport and Brecon line platforms at Talyllyn West Junction with the 12.10pm Brecon to Newport train. On the right-hand side can be seen the fingerposts for the Hereford and Moat Lane platform. Talyllyn Junction was three-sided, thus allowing trains from Hereford and Mid Wales direct access to the Brecon and Merthyr lines.

The only feature of the 'past' picture that remains in today's scene, photographed on 4 March 1998, is the house at the extreme right of the picture, now almost obscured by trees. *Hugh Ballantyne/RS*

BRECON: Ex-GWR 0-6-0 pannier tank No 9616 arrives at Brecon on 28 December 1962 with the penultimate 8.03am train from Newport. Sadly, all Brecon lines were to close by 30 December, on which day the SLS ran a 'Farewell to the Brecon lines of the former Cambrian and Midland Railways' special. The line from Talyllyn to Brecon opened in 1863, and was originally operated by the Brecon & Merthyr Railway (B&M), then by the Midland Railway.

Today's scene, photographed on 4 March 1998, shows that the station and its fine-looking station house have all gone long ago and there is nothing now to indicate that the railway was here at all. *Hugh Ballantyne/RS*

TALYBONT ON USK: We finish our journey in this area here on the Brecon & Merthyr line, about 4 miles south of Talyllyn Junction. This view of Talybont on Usk station, looking north, was taken in the early 1960s.

The present view, taken on 4 March 1998, shows the station house still intact and now used as an outdoor education centre, while the platform seems to be in good order. *Lens of Sutton/RS*

Interlude: Preserved steam on the Cambrian and Marches routes

As mentioned earlier, the Welsh Marches played host to the return of main-line steam back in October 197I, and since then there have been many hundreds of steam specials along this picturesque route.

It was not until the late spring of 1987 that steam returned to the Cambrian lines, but, unlike the Marches, not on a semi-regular basis. Nowadays only DMUs are allowed to cross Barmouth bridge, so steam specials usually terminate at Towyn on the Barmouth line.

The following is a selection of pictures taken on both routes over the years.

Ex-Southern Railway 'Lord Nelson' Class 4-6-0 No 850 *Lord Nelson* is now no longer seen on the main line, but on 13 June 1981 headed south near All Stretton with a Chester to Hereford special, the 'Cathedrals Pullman'. *RS*

On 24 June 1990 ex-GWR 'King' Class 4-6-0 No 6024 *King Edward I* races through Woofferton (formerly Woofferton Junction) with a Newport-Shrewsbury special. *RS*

Above Double-chimneyed ex-LMS 'Jubilee' Class 4-6-0 No 45596 *Bahamas* climbs the 1 in 130/150 out of Craven Arms with a northbound 'Welsh Marches Express' on 3 August 1991. *RS*

Below Now on the Cambrian line we see BR Standard Class 4-6-0 No 75069 threading the pleasant Welsh countryside west of Newtown with a Shrewsbury to Aberystwyth train on 22 September 1991. *RS*

Approaching Aberdovey, near Trefi, on 25 May 1987 is a Severn Valley locomotive, ex-GWR 'Manor' Class 4-6-0 No 7819 *Hinton Manor*, with the 1340 Machynlleth-Barmouth train. *RS*

No 7819 *Hinton Manor* is seen again with a fine rake of GWR coaches taking the Barmouth road at Dovey Junction with the 0940 Machynlleth-Barmouth train on the same day. This was the second day of the return of main-line steam to the Cambrian line, with return workings each day spread over the Whitsun holiday week. The Aberystwyth lines are on the right-hand side. *RS*

On the first day – 24 May 1987 – of that historic return to steam working on the Cambrian, No 7819 crosses Barmouth bridge with the 1445 Machynlleth-Barmouth train. A telephoto lens accentuates the Cader Idris mountain range. *RS*

Some four years later, on 23 June 1991, No 75069 hugs the Cambrian coastline near Frongoch with a Barmouth to Shrewsbury special. *RS*

Hinton Manor closes this interlude, heading out of Newtown with a Shrewsbury-Barmouth charter on 16 June 1991. *RS*

Cambrian route: Shrewsbury to Welshpool

SUTTON BRIDGE JUNCTION: We start our journey on the Cambrian route back at Sutton Bridge Junction, Shrewsbury, with a reminder of locomotive-hauled travel on the Aberystwyth trains. Nowadays we only see 'Sprinter' units on passenger workings, but on 26 August 1989 Class 37 Nos 37029 and 37030 are seen coming off the Cambrian line on to the North & West route with the Summer Saturday 12-coach 1013 Aberystwyth-Euston train. It will take the Shrewsbury avoiding line at Foregate Junction to continue its journey to Wolverhampton and the south.

Although we refer to the Cambrian route as having run from Shrewsbury in pre-Grouping days, the 17 miles from Shrewsbury to Buttington Junction were in fact owned jointly by the GWR and LNWR, the line joining the Cambrian Railways route from Whitchurch/Oswestry to Welshpool and the coast at Buttington Junction. *RS*

MEOLE BRACE: On 24 September 1960 ex-GWR '9000' ('Dukedog') Class 4-4-0 No 9017 and '4300' Class 2-6-0 No 7330 double-head the Talyllyn Railway special from Paddington to Towyn at Meole Brace on the outskirts of Shrewsbury. Although the inside-cylindered 'Dukedogs' had a late-Victorian look about them, like the 'Duke' Class 4-4-0s of 1895, they were not introduced until 1936, and worked mainly on the Cambrian lines. No 9017 is preserved on the Bluebell Railway and is named *Earl of Berkeley*.

On 31 March 1998 DMU No 150130 heads downgrade through Meole Brace with the 0802 Pwllheli-Shrewsbury-Birmingham New Street service. Apart from the singling of the track, very little seems to have changed in 38 years. *Michael Mensing/RS*

HANWOOD, some 5 miles west of Shrewsbury, was the junction for the 5-mile branch to Minsterley (to the south-west). This branch opened in 1861 but closed to passengers in 1951 and was closed completely in 1965. At Pontesbury on the branch was an exchange siding for the industrial line to Snailbeach lead mine to the south. On 9 July 1966 the down 'Cambrian Coast Express' (2.15pm from Shrewsbury), hauled by Standard Class '4' 2-6-0 No 76038, heads westwards through Hanwood. The divergence of the Minsterley branch (although closed the year before) can be seen clearly.

By 31 March 1998 everything is overgrown. Beyond the trees can be seen No 158849 with the 1017 Birmingham New Street-Aberystwyth service. The Minsterley branch was taken up long ago. *Michael Mensing/RS*

YOCKLETON: Standard Class '4' 4-6-0 climbs the 1 in 100 at Yockleton, 8 miles west of Shrewsbury, with the down 'Cambrian' on 29 October 1966. A few months later, on 4 March 1967, with the end of the through workings from Paddington, steam would finish on the Cambrian lines.

At the same location on 31 March 1998 very little can be seen of the 1637 Birmingham New Street-Aberystwyth train. *Both RS*

WESTBURY: This 21 April 1962 photograph was taken from the 8.05am Shrewsbury to Aberystwyth train, hauled by ex-GWR 2-6-0 No 6378, as it ran through Westbury station. The incoming train, hauled by sister engine No 7336, is the 6.30am from Machynlleth to Shrewsbury.

On 31 March 1998 the station house is in private use and automatic barriers have replaced the old gates and signal box. *Michael Mensing/RS*

BREIDDEN (MIDDLETOWN): On Saturday 6 August 1966 Standard Class '4' 4-6-0 No 75002 climbs the 1 in 53 towards Breidden (formerly Middletown) with the 7.30am Pwllheli to Birmingham train. No 75002 was built in 1951 and withdrawn from service in August 1967.

By 31 March 1998 the whole area has become very overgrown, and 'Sprinter' No 159851 forming the 1217 Birmingham New Street to Aberystwyth service can barely be seen through the trees that have grown up over the ensuing 32 years. *Both RS*

NEAR TREWERN: The up 'Cambrian' with 4-6-0 No 75029 in charge climbs the 1 in 80 near Trewern on Tuesday 25 October 1966. The line is now in Wales, the border between Shropshire and what was Montgomeryshire being some 2 miles east of this location. In the background of the right-hand pictures is Breidden Hill, and the hedgerow in the middle distance hides the A458 Shrewsbury to Welshpool road.

Except for the motive power, a few new houses and the usual growth of trees and bushes, nothing appears to have changed at this location as the 1330 (left) and 1417 Birmingham New Street to Aberystwyth services pass on 31 March 1998. *All RS*

BUTTINGTON JUNCTION, 3 miles west of Welshpool, was where the Joint line from Shrewsbury met the Cambrian line proper. On 5 March 1956 Standard Class '4' No 75005 passes through the station non-stop with the 9.45am from Whitchurch to Aberystwyth, while ex-GWR 0-6-0 No 3207 stands by the signal box with a permanent way train. The lines from Shrewsbury are on the right.

The line from Whitchurch to Buttington Junction was closed in 1965, and it is very difficult to imagine from this view, taken on 31 March 1998, that there was once a busy junction station at this location. *Hugh Ballantyne/RS*

WELSHPOOL: These next two scenes show that major changes have taken place at Welshpool. On the late afternoon of 31 March 1962, the down 'Cambrian Coast Express', comprising ex-GWR 'Manor' Class 4-6-0 No 7823 *Hook Norton Manor* and a fine rake of chocolate-and-cream coaches, pauses both for passengers and, as can be seen, for the locomotive to take water. The train left Paddington at 11.10am and will take around 6 hours to reach Aberystwyth.

Today's picture shows that the elegant station building has been preserved as a craft centre and that the old main line is now part of a bypass route. The new station, consisting of one island platform, is roughly where the former goods yard was. Approaching the new station exactly 36 years later, on 31 March 1998, is No 158851 forming the 1529 Aberystwyth to Birmingham New Street service. *Hugh Ballantyne/RS*

Welshpool and Llanfair Light Railway

While in Welshpool we will pause to take a look at the Welshpool & Llanfair Light Railway. This narrow-gauge (2ft 6in) line was opened from Welshpool to Llanfair Caereinion in 1903. The 9-mile route, although independent, was worked by the Cambrian and then the GWR, and finally by BR. Passenger services finished in 1931, but freight traffic continued until the line was closed in November 1956. However, as most enthusiasts know, a preservation society was formed and the line was re-opened in 1963. This line, together with the Vale of Rheidol Railway and possibly the Fairbourne & Barmouth Railway, will be the subject of a future 'Past and Present Companion' volume.

WELSHPOOL RAVEN SQUARE: On 24 May 1987 the 1220 to Llanfair departs from the then newly built Welshpool Raven Square station. Double-heading the train are locomotives Nos 85 (ex-Sierra Leone Railway 2-6-2T built by Hunslet in 1954) and 0-6-0T No 823 *The Countess*. No 823 and No 822 *The Earl* were the original two engines built for the line by Beyer Peacock in 1902. The station building at Raven Square (out of sight in this view) was previously at Eardisley on the Hereford-Brecon line (see page 57). *RS*

Opposite page **SMITHFIELD ROAD, WELSHPOOL: Flashback to 1 June 1956, a few months before the closure of the W&LLR. No 822 *The Earl* shunts coal wagons across Smithfield Road prior to leaving for Llanfair. Welshpool station is in the background. The second photograph shows the same scene on 31 March 1998.** *Hugh Ballantyne RS*

Above BANWY BRIDGE: In the first of two further scenes from the preservation era No 10 *Sir Drefaldwyn* (a 1944 Franco-Belge ex-German Wermacht 0-8-0T) crosses Banwy bridge with a Llanfair train on 9 July 1972. The bridge crosses the River Vernwy, 3 miles east of Llanfair Caereinion station. *RS*

Below LLANFAIR CAEREINION: *The Earl* shunts stock at Llanfair station for the first train of the day on 20 April 1973. *RS*

Cambrian route: Welshpool to Builth Road

ABERMULE was the junction for the short (3⅝ miles) branch to Kerry. Opened in 1863, it closed to passenger traffic in 1931, freight traffic in 1956, and was dismantled in 1959. The main freight was coal, timber, fertiliser and sheep during the September sales. Just west of Abermule, 10 miles from Welshpool, BR Standard Class '4' 2-6-0 No 76037 heads towards the coast with the 'Cambrian Coast Express' on 25 June 1966.

On 18 April 1998 it is almost impossible to see anything of the 1129 Aberystwyth-Birmingham New Street service. *Michael Mensing/RS*

NEWTOWN: From Buttington Junction westwards, the line was originally owned by the Cambrian Railways. Shrewsbury to Buttington was opened in 1862, but the line from Buttington to Welshpool, connecting that town with Oswestry, was opened earlier in 1860, as was the line to Newtown and Llanidloes via Moat Lane Junction. On 12 August 1983 a three-car DMU set, forming the 1646 Shrewsbury to Aberystwyth service, departs from Newtown station. At this date Newtown still had a signal box and semaphore signals, and a goods loop on the right-hand side.

By 16 April 1998 the signal box, semaphore signals and goods loop have all gone. The train is the 1017 Birmingham New Street to Aberystwyth service formed of 'Sprinter' unit No 158795. *Both RS*

MOAT LANE JUNCTION: As can be seen from this picture, taken on 7 June 1960, Moat Lane Junction was a very busy and important junction station. From left to right, we see Class '2MT' 2-6-0 No 46521 (in lined green livery) shunting; sister engine No 46523 waiting with the stock of the 5.40pm to Builth Wells; the rear of the 2.30pm Aberystwyth to Oswestry train hauled by ex-GWR 'Manor' Class 4-6-0 No 7801 *Anthony Manor*; and finally BR Standard Class '2MT' 2-6-0 No 78002 on the 4.20pm Newtown to Machynlleth service. The line to Llanidloes and Builth Wells (and on to Three Cocks Junction and Brecon) runs at the back of the station building, so No 46523 will have to reverse its empty stock, then pull into the Brecon platform on the other side of the station before picking up passengers for the journey to Builth Wells.

At the site of the former Moat Lane Junction on 18 April 1998 No 158794 approaches with the 1217 Birmingham New Street-Aberystwyth service. What a contrast! *Hugh Ballantyne/RS*

LLANIDLOES: From Moat Lane Junction we briefly leave the coast line and join No 46523 and the 5.40pm Builth Wells train on 7 June 1960 for a trip on the Mid-Wales line, calling first at the impressive-looking station at Llanidloes. Apart from the fine station building, note the locomotive shed, goods shed, sidings, etc, all part of a busy railway scene. It was rumoured that Llanidloes would be the HQ of the Cambrian Railway, a probable explanation for the size of the station buildings. In the event, that distinction went to Oswestry.

Llanidloes today presents a very different picture, with the town bypass now occupying the railway trackbed. However, the station building is still there, now in private use and looking in very good order. This picture was taken on 18 April 1998. *Hugh Ballantyne/RS*

BUILTH WELLS LOWER: On 21 April 1962 Class '2MT' 2-6-0 No 46515 leaves Builth Wells Lower with the 1.20pm Brecon to Moat Lane Junction service. The photograph was taken from Builth Road Upper station, through which ran the Central Wales line from Craven Arms to Swansea. This line is the subject of a separate 'Past and Present Companion' volume.

The second picture shows the site of Builth Road Lower station on 7 March 1998. Although the line closed in 1962, the station buildings on the left, not seen in the 'past' picture, are still in use as a public house and a private dwelling. *Michael Mensing/RS*

Cambrian Coast: Moat Lane to Dovey Junction

CAERSWS is over a mile from Moat Lane Junction. Although the coast route was mainly single track from Shrewsbury to Newtown, from Newtown to Moat Lane Junction it was double track, then from Moat Lane to Machynlleth it was once again single. Caersws was the junction for the branch to Garth Road and Van to the south-west, which closed in 1940. Also at Caersws the River Severn, which the line has followed from Welshpool, now heads south, and the Cambrian line to Machynlleth and the coast turns to the north-west. On 13 August 1983 Class 25 Nos 25276 and 25284 pause with the 1400 Aberystwyth-Shrewsbury train (Saturdays only) for the exchange of the single-line tokens.

Some 15 years later, on 18 April 1998, No 158381 stops at Caersws with the 1330 Aberystwyth-Birmingham New Street service. The crossing gates are still worked by hand, but the passing loop has been removed and subsequently the semaphore signals on the left-hand side. *Both RS*

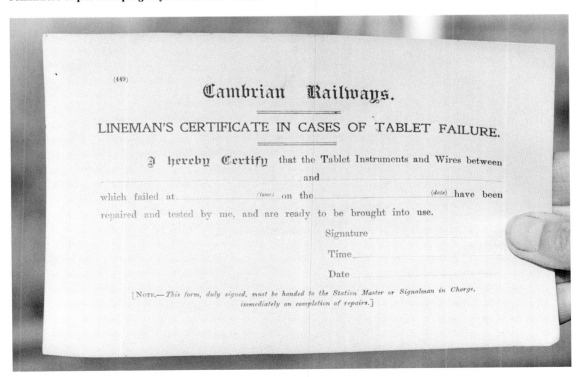

(377)

CAMBRIAN RAILWAYS.

Station,   19

Failure in Tablet Working

*Between*_____ *and*_____

I have to report that a failure occurred to-day in the Tablet Working on the above section, particulars of which are given below:—

Station at which failure occurred

Exact time of failure

Date and exact time Tablet Working restored

Nature of failure

	No. of Train.	Period of Delay. H. M.	Station at which delayed.
Trains delayed in consequence } of failure.			

How Traffic was worked while failure lasted

REMARKS (to be continued on back when necessary):

_____ Station Master.

This Form is to be carefully and fully filled up by the Station Master at each end of the Section on which the failure occurred, and sent to the Superintendent of Line's Office by the first train after the occurrence of any Tablet failure in addition to the usual Telegraphic Advice.

While at Caersws in 1983 I was invited into the signal box and shown these Cambrian Railways forms, interesting reminders of pre-Grouping days on the line. *Both RS*

---

(449)

Cambrian Railways.

LINEMAN'S CERTIFICATE IN CASES OF TABLET FAILURE.

I hereby Certify that the Tablet Instruments and Wires between

_____ and _____

which failed at_____ *(time)* on the_____ *(date)* have been

repaired and tested by me, and are ready to be brought into use.

Signature_____

Time_____

Date_____

[NOTE.— *This form, duly signed, must be handed to the Station Master or Signalman in Charge, immediately on completion of repairs.*]

TALERDDIG station was 8 miles from Caersws at the summit of a 13-mile climb for eastbound trains from Machynlleth, the final 4 miles of which were at 1 in 52. For westbound trains from Caersws it is an easier climb, the steepest grade being 1 in 100. This view of the eastern end of Talerddig station was taken on 4 March 1967, the last day of steam workings on the line.

On 18 April 1998 there is very little left to compare with the 'past' view – only the passing loop and the crossing. The station house survives (now in private use) out of the picture on the right. *Michael Mensing/RS*

TALERDDIG BANK (1): On a glorious summer Saturday, 20 August 1966, BR Standard Class '4MT' 4-6-0s Nos 75O19 and 75020 climb the last mile of the 1 in 52 of Talerddig bank with the 10.55am Pwllheli-Birmingham Snow Hill train.
   On 23 June 1991 the same scene is re-enacted with 4-6-0 No 75069 hauling a Barmouth-Shrewsbury special train. *Both RS*

TALERDDIG BANK (2): At the same location on Saturday 16 June 1990 Class 37 No 37427 thunders up the bank (the train could be heard approaching for several miles) with the 0932 Pwllheli to Euston train. This was the last year for locomotive-hauled passenger trains on the Cambrian.

The line now sees only DMUs; here No 158794 climbs up Talerddig on 18 April 1998 forming the 1529 Aberystwyth-Birmingham New Street service. Note how since the days of BR steam the lineside has become very overgrown. However, the bridge over the A470 can still be seen in the later picture. *Both RS*

MACHYNLLETH (1): The line, having passed through Cemmaes Road, the junction for the Dinas Mawddwy branch that closed in 1950, arrives at the major town of Machynlleth. Although Dovey Junction is the diverging point for the Aberystwyth and Barmouth/Pwllheli routes, because of its inaccessibility (it is difficult to get to by road) Machynlleth is usually regarded as the junction station, certainly for travellers other than from Barmouth to Aberystwyth and vice versa. There was also a locomotive shed here, and even today there is a small maintenance depot for the units that operate the line. On the evening of Saturday 16 June 1990 Class 37 No 37427 enters Machynlleth with the 1530 service from Euston, the down 'Cambrian'. On the right is the locomotive shed extension, beyond which is the shed itself.

On the evening of 18 April 1998 'Sprinter' No 158795 forms the 1637 Birmingham New Street to Aberystwyth service. The shed extension has been demolished, and the old shed building has been converted into a small diesel maintenance depot. However, all the semaphore signals are as they were in the 'past' picture. *Both RS*

MACHYNLLETH (2): Around 1900 Cambrian Railways locomotive No 43 stands in the down platform at Machynlleth. Note the sign on the left giving directions to the Corris Railway station; this narrow-gauge line ran north from Machynlleth to Aberllefeni, a distance of around 7 miles. It opened fully in 1887, but closed to passengers in 1931, and completely in 1948.

A century or so later, on 18 April 1998, unit No 156401 leaves Machynlleth with the 1706 to Aberystwyth. Obviously many things have changed over that period of time, although the main station building (with a few modifications) looks much the same. *Lens of Sutton/RS*

DOVEY JUNCTION (1): It is early mid-morning on Saturday 13 August 1983, and Class 25 Nos 25181 and 25229 approach Dovey Junction with the 0700 Shrewsbury to Aberystwyth train.

The second picture was taken a short while later on the same day, as a three-car DMU approaches the Barmouth line platform with the 0921 Machynlleth to Pwllheli service. Both these pictures show clearly the junction layout and the abundance of semaphore signals at this rather isolated junction station.

Today's picture shows how the junction has been rationalised; indeed, it is really a junction no more, just two lines – the left to Barmouth and the right to Aberystwyth. The rear of the 1746 Aberystwyth to Birmingham New Street service formed of 'Sprinter' unit No 158836 together with the colour light signals controlled from Machynlleth complete the scene on 18 April 1998. *All RS*

DOVEY JUNCTION (2): Turning round from the previous pictures, we have this very pleasant view of Dovey Junction station on 9 June 1960. On the left, just arrived from Aberystwyth, is ex-GWR 'Manor' Class 4-6-0 No 7818 *Erlestoke Manor* (now preserved by the Great Western Society at Didcot) on the up 'Cambrian Coast Express'. On the right is ex-GWR 2-6-0 No 6392 on the Pwllheli connecting train, and on the extreme right is ex-GWR 0-6-0 No 2217.

The 'present' picture, taken on 18 April 1998, shows unit No 158856 forming the 1746 Aberystwyth to Birmingham New Street service, and also the many changes from the 'past' view. The loop lines and semaphore signals have gone, new lamps and platform buildings have replaced the old ones, and the platform itself has been resurfaced and widened. *Hugh Ballantyne/RS*

Dovey Junction to Barmouth

ABERDOVEY: From Dovey Junction, first of all we take the northern route to Barmouth, which for most of its 21 miles runs close to the Cambrian coastline. Some 6 miles from Dovey Junction is the attractive coastal resort of Aberdovey; this view of the station, looking towards Barmouth, was taken in the late 1950s.

On 27 April 1998 the station building is still intact, but very little else in comparison with the earlier picture. Also, a 'bus shelter' has been added to the side of the station buildings. *Lens of Sutton/RS*

TOWYN is a coastal resort 3.5 miles north of Aberdovey, and on the evening of 30 August 1959 ex-GWR 0-6-0 No 3209 is seen pulling into the station with a return Barmouth-Wolverhampton-Birmingham and Tyseley excursion train. Excursions from Birmingham on the Western Region often started from Tyseley, which was where the main carriage sidings were located.

A comparison with today's picture, taken on 27 April 1998, shows that the main station buildings are still intact but out of use – nowadays tickets are obtained on the train. Also the 'past' picture was taken from the station footbridge, which is now long gone. The train is the 1152 Barmouth-Machynlleth service with No 153334. *Michael Mensing/RS*

TALYLLYN RAILWAY: Among its many attractions, Towyn is also the headquarters of the famous Talyllyn narrow-gauge (2ft 3in) railway. This railway is the subject of a separate 'Past and Present Companion' volume, but as a reminder of this delightful line I have included this picture of ex-Corris Railway 0-4-2ST No 3 *Sir Haydn* (built in 1878) as it crosses Dolgoch viaduct on 27 April 1973 with the 2.30pm Towyn to Abergynolwyn train. *RS*

Left FAIRBOURNE & BARMOUTH RAILWAY (1): At Fairbourne, some 3 miles south of Barmouth, and adjacent to the Cambrian line is the Fairbourne & Barmouth Railway, which runs to Porth Penrhyn on the Mawddach estuary, where there is a ferry crossing to Barmouth. Today this is a 10¼-inch-gauge railway, but from 1916 until the mid-1980s it was a 15-inch-gauge line. This picture, taken on 7 August 1973, shows one of the fine 15-inch-gauge locomotives, *Ernest W. Twining*, waiting to leave with the 6pm train to the ferry. This locomotive (which was in light blue livery) was built by Basset-Lowke in 1949 and rebuilt in 1966. The station building behind also served as the engine shed. *RS*

Opposite page FAIRBOURNE & BARMOUTH RAILWAY (2): It is the end of the day's workings on the line and *Katie*, a 2-4-2 locomotive built in the early 1960s, marshals the empty stock of the last train on 24 April 1973.

The similar view taken on 27 April 1998 shows the line's smart stock. After 25 years the Harlequin cafe still appears to be going strong. An added attraction at Fairbourne today is the Rowen Indoor Nature Centre, situated next to the railway. *Both RS*

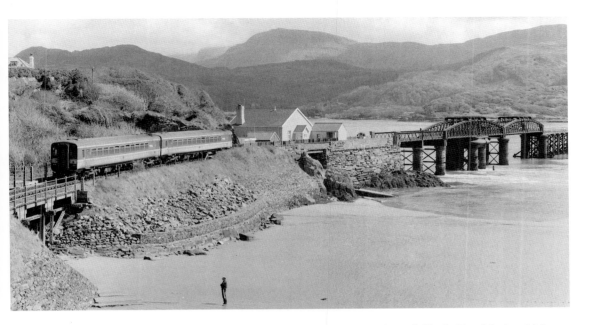

BARMOUTH BRIDGE: After leaving Fairbourne the Cambrian line passes through Morfa Mawddach, which was the junction for the line from Dolgelly and Ruabon. Although this line closed completely in 1968, happily the section from Llangollen to Carrog has been preserved, and is known as the Llangollen Railway. Less than a mile from Morfa Mawddach is the famous Barmouth bridge across the Mawddach estuary. On 24 May 1987 ex-GWR 'Manor' Class 4-6-0 No 7819 *Hinton Manor* heads off the bridge with the 1445 from Machynlleth to Barmouth. This end of the bridge has a swinging section, originally to allow river traffic up to Dolgelly, but it is many years since this was in general use.

In the early to mid-1980s there were weight restrictions on the bridge, only allowing diesel units across. These restrictions were lifted at the end of the 1980s, and on the 16 June 1990 Class 37 No 37431 is seen coming off the bridge with the 0903 Euston to Pwllheli train.

Weight restrictions were re-imposed on bridge traffic in the early 1990s, and nowadays once again only units are allowed access. On 27 April 1998 No 153365 is seen forming the 1250 Machynlleth to Pwllheli service. Also note that both pedestrians and pedal cyclists can cross the mile-long bridge by the walkway that runs parallel to the track, but that this is subject to a toll. *All RS*

Below The bridge seen from a different angle. *Hinton Manor* is once again the locomotive, this time with the 1530 Barmouth to Machynlleth train on 25 May 1987. *RS*

BARMOUTH (1): A vintage scene at Barmouth, taken probably in the 1930s, with GWR '14XX' Class 0-4-2 No 1430 on a push-pull train in the bay platform at the southern end of the station. At the main station platform is an ex-Cambrian Railways 0-6-0 on a local stopping train, probably to Machynlleth.

Today's scene shows that although the buildings surrounding the station have been changed only cosmetically, the bay platform and much of the trackwork has long since gone, as well as the footbridge over the level crossing, but the station building survives. The rear of the 1422 Machynlleth-Pwllheli service (unit No 156409) can be seen heading into the station on 27 April 1998. *Lens of Sutton/RS*

BARMOUTH (2): This view of the southern end of Barmouth station looking towards Machynlleth was taken in the late 1950s from the footbridge over the level crossing. In the bay platform is ex-GWR 'Manor' Class 4-6-0 No 7811 *Dunley Manor*.

The 27 April 1998 view had to be taken from ground level. A modern crossing has replaced the old gates, but the signal box is still there, although now out of use and probably destined for preservation. Most of the 'past' buildings survive, with a few new additions. Happily, the brick base of the footbridge now accommodates the shop outlet of an excellent bread and cakes business, whose bakehouse stands immediately behind. *Lens of Sutton/RS*

Dovey Junction to Aberystwyth and beyond

DOVEY JUNCTION: We return to Dovey Junction to continue our journey to Aberystwyth and beyond. On 13 August 1983 Class 25 Nos 25181 and 25229 enter the Aberystwyth platform with the Saturdays-only 0900 Shrewsbury to Aberystwyth train. For technical reasons I was unable to duplicate this scene with a present-day equivalent; please refer to page 105 for a modern comparison. It will be seen that today the loop line has gone, together with the semaphore signals; the somewhat utilitarian-looking station buildings have also been replaced with a more graceful design.

The second photograph shows another pair of Class 25s, Nos 25284 and 25276, leaving Dovey Junction with the 0945 Wolverhampton to Aberystwyth train on the same day.
Both RS

BORTH: For the 9 miles from Dovey Junction to Borth the line follows the estuary of the River Dovey, but for the final 8 miles to Aberystwyth the line runs inland except for the last 2 miles to Aberystwyth, when it swings west to the coast and the station, where it terminates, 81.5 miles from Shrewsbury and 234.5 from Paddington. This view of the station at the seaside resort of Borth, looking west, was taken on 23 August 1905, and shows well the single platform.

At a first glance at the 'present' picture taken on 27 April 1998, one could be forgiven for thinking that time had stood still. However, a further glance shows that the canopy his been shortened at both ends, and a few chimneys have gone, but not much has altered superficially over nearly 100 years. *J. A. Peden collection/RS*

ABERYSTWYTH MPD (1): Just before Aberystwyth station when approaching from the east was the locomotive shed, situated in the fork of the Machynlleth and Carmarthen lines, the latter coming in from the south. On 17 May 1955 the visitor would have been greeted by the splendid sight of three ex-GWR 'Dukedog' 4-4-0s, Nos 9027, 9017 and 9021.

Today the shed is used by the narrow-gauge Vale of Rheidol locomotives. The line to Devil's Bridge can be seen on the left, and on the right, where there were once carriage sidings, etc, there is just the single line from Machynlleth, plus a loop line. The date is 27 April 1998. *Brian Moone/RS*

ABERYSTWYTH MPD (2): This view of the other end of the shed dates from the early 1960s, and shows the Machynlleth line on the left and the Carmarthen line swinging away on the right.

By 27 April 1998 all the shed area and the old Carmarthen side are used by the Vale of Rheidol Railway. The original terminus of this 1ft 11½in gauge line was south of this location, but was moved to the main-line station in 1968. The line was opened in 1902, and at the end of main-line steam in August 1968 it was unique in being BR's only steam-operated line. *Lens of Sutton/RS*

ABERYSTWYTH: On 1 August 1960 ex-GWR '4300' Class 2-6-0 No 5369 waits to leave Aberystwyth with the 5.50pm return excursion to Birmingham Snow Hill and Tyseley.

Today Aberystwyth has just one platform and a run-round loop. Waiting to leave the modernised station on 27 April 1998 is single-car unit No 153334 forming the 0925 for Machynlleth. Note the platforms on the left for the Vale of Rheidol trains. *Michael Mensing/RS*

VALE OF RHEIDOL RAILWAY: The Vale of Rheidol Railway is to be the subject of a future 'Past and Present Companion', but I have included this picture of 2-6-2T No 9 *Prince of Wales* approaching Devil's Bridge on 9 August 1973 with the 2.15pm Aberystwyth-Devil's Bridge train as a reminder of this attractive 11.75-mile narrow-gauge railway. *RS*

STATA FLORIDA: We are now on the Aberystwyth to Carmarthen route at Strata Florida station, 15.25 miles from Aberystwyth, serving Ystrad Meurig village, among others. It gained its name from the nearby abbey ruins, and as can be seen from this picture, taken on 9 June 1960, the station was not only a crossing point on the line but also had a small goods yard, mainly, probably, for sheep traffic. On the left is an Aberystwyth-bound train crossing ex-GWR 2-6-0 No 6310 on the 11.55am Aberystwyth to Carmarthen train; on the right another '63XX; shunts vans. The line from Strata Florida to Aberystwyth opened in 1867, and closed in 1964.

The house seen in the 'present' view taken on 26 April 1998 can just be glimpsed above the final coach of the Aberystwyth train in the 'past' picture. The hillside also identifies the location. *Hugh Ballantyne/RS*

ABERAYRON: Leaving the Carmarthen line just north of Lampeter was the 12-mile branch to the seaside resort of Aberayron, which opened in 1911. The passenger service finished in 1951, so this scene of the branch train at this westerly terminus was probably taken in the late 1940s.

It is very difficult to guess, looking at the second picture, taken on 24 April 1998, that there was a station at this location, but I can confirm that the white cottages seen in the 'past' picture are still there to give positive identification of the site. *Lens of Sutton/RS*

PENCADER: At Pencader in the late 1950s is ex-GWR 'Manor' Class 4-6-0 No 7826 *Longworth Manor*, on an Aberystwyth to Carmarthen train, together with a pannier tank with a southbound goods waiting to leave after the passenger.

At the site of Pencader station on 26 April 1998 only the background hills provide a link with the 'past' scene. Although all the lines in this area closed in 1973, just south of Pencader a section of the Carmarthen line from Bronwydd Arms to Llwyfan has been preserved, and is known as the Gwili Railway. *Lens of Sutton/RS*

NEWCASTLE EMLYN: To the west from Pencader ran the branch to Newcastle Emlyn, which closed to passenger traffic in 1952, but which continued to handle freight until 1973. Looking at the motor vehicles, I would guess that this picture of the terminus was taken probably in the early 1960s. Today the site is, among other things, a car storage depot, but the hillside and some of the houses correspond with the 'past' picture. *Lens of Sutton/RS*

INDEX OF LOCATIONS